TUTANKHAMUN

THE LIFE AND DEATH OF A
PHARAOH

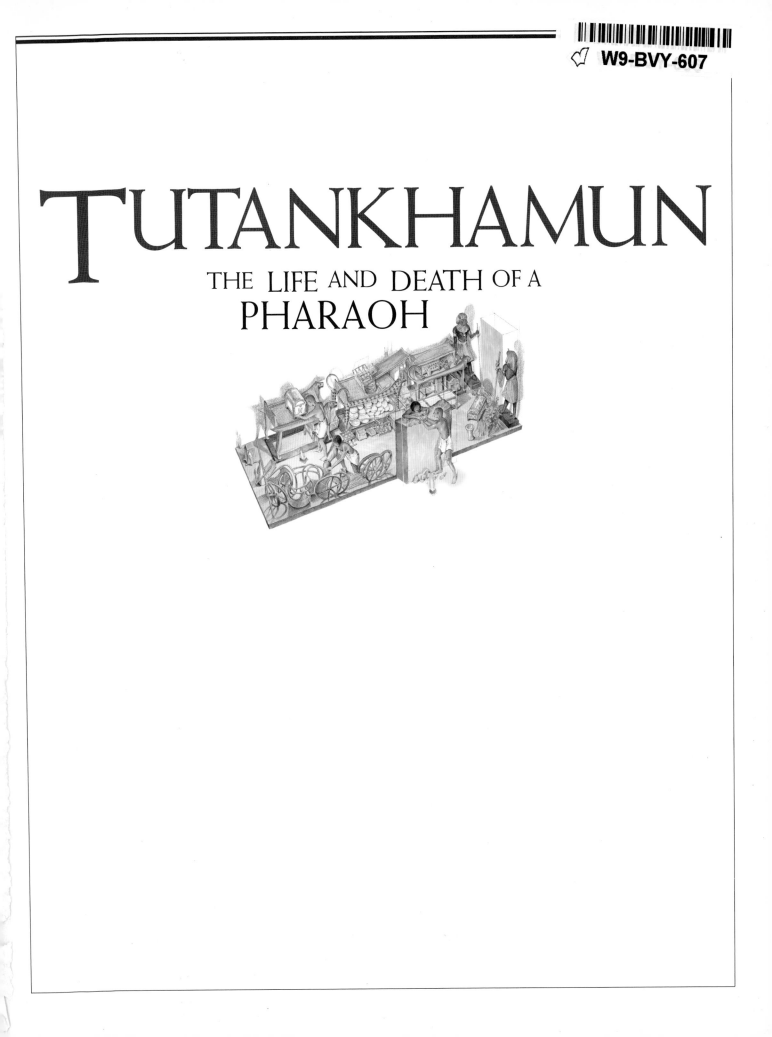

Tutankhamun's mummy was enclosed in three coffins, a sarcophagus, and four shrines.

Assembling the canopic shrine

Howard Carter and his team look into the tomb for the first time.

The blue crown

The *nemes* head cloth

The double crown

The treasury of Tutankhamun's tomb

TUTANKHAMUN

THE LIFE AND DEATH OF A
PHARAOH

Written by
DAVID MURDOCH

Illustrated by
CHRIS FORSEY
ANNE YVONNE GILBERT
ERIC THOMAS

DORLING KINDERSLEY
LONDON • NEW YORK • MOSCOW • SYDNEY

DK

LONDON, NEW YORK, MUNICH, MELBOURNE and DELHI

Project Editor Susan Malyan
Art Editor Penny Lamprell
Senior Editor Scarlett O'Hara
Senior Art Editor Vicky Wharton
Senior Managing Editor Linda Martin
Senior Managing Art Editor Julia Harris
DTP Designer Almudena Díaz
Picture Research Catherine Edkins
Jacket Designer Mark Haygarth
Production Lisa Moss

Hardback edition first published in Great Britain in 1998
This edition published in Great Britain in 2003
by Dorling Kindersley Limited,
80 Strand, London, WC2R 0RL

2 4 6 8 10 9 7 5 3 1

A CIP catalogue record for this book is available
from the British Library.

ISBN 0 7513 3748 X

Reproduced by Colourscan, Singapore
Printed and bound by L.E.G.O., Italy

Additional illustrations by John Lawrence

Quotes from *The Tomb of Tutankhamun* by Howard Carter
Copyright © The Griffith Institute,
Ashmolean Museum, Oxford

see our complete
catalogue at
www.dk.com

Contents

The Discovery

W HEN ARCHAEOLOGIST Howard Carter shone his torch through a hole in the door of Tutankhamun's tomb, this was the amazing sight that met his eyes. Hundreds of priceless treasures were piled up inside, waiting to be discovered.

" EYEWITNESS

"We had worked for months at a stretch and found nothing.... We had almost made up our minds that we were beaten, and were preparing to leave the Valley; and then – hardly had we set hoe to ground in our last despairing effort than we made a discovery that far exceeded our wildest dreams."

Howard Carter and Arthur Mace, from their book *The Tomb of Tutankhamun,* 1923–33

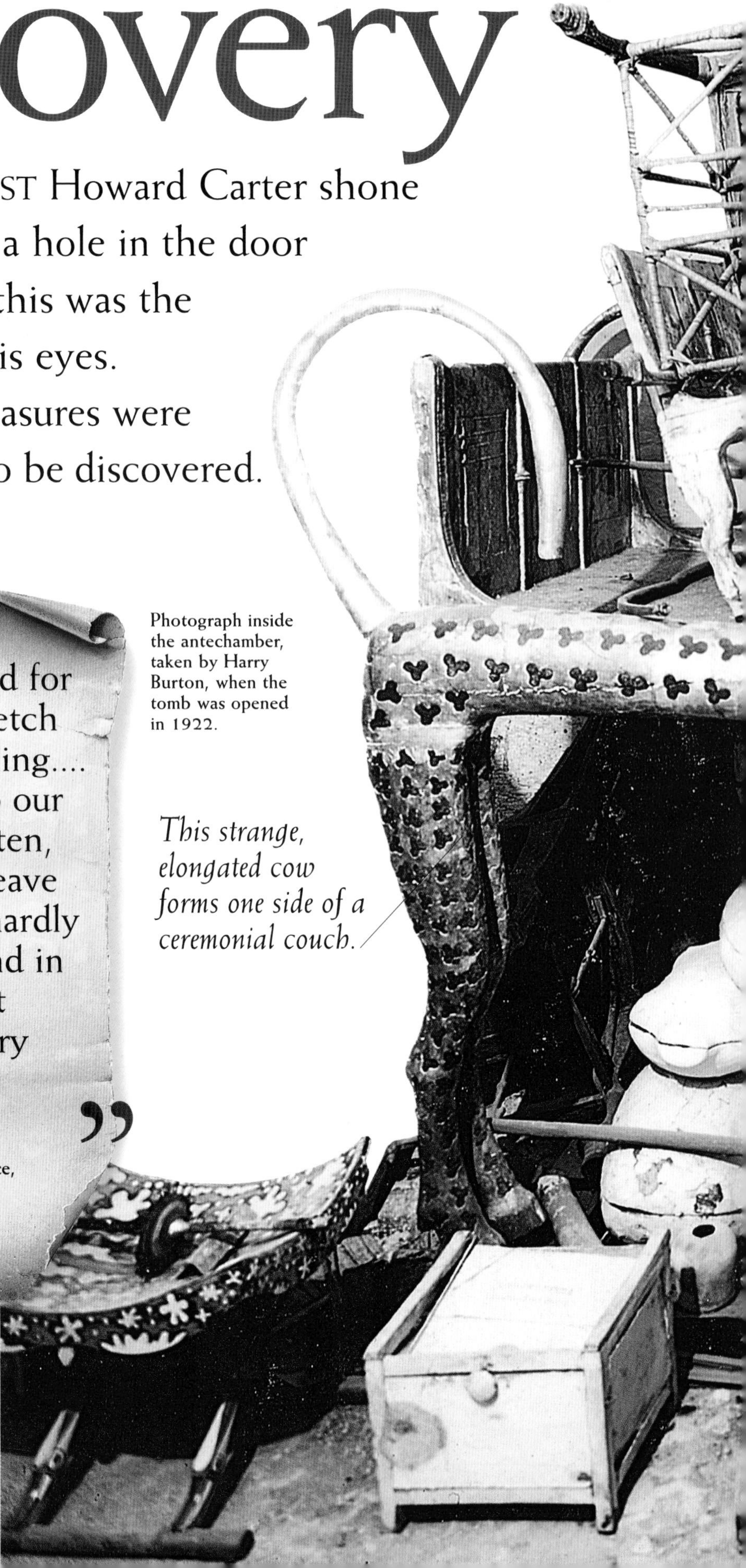

"

Photograph inside the antechamber, taken by Harry Burton, when the tomb was opened in 1922.

This strange, elongated cow forms one side of a ceremonial couch.

This is one of six beds found in the tomb. Like all the treasures, they were put there for Tutankhamun to use in the afterlife.

THE CHARACTERS

MORE THAN 3,000 YEARS separate the two casts of characters shown on these pages. In 1327 BC, Tutankhamun, pharaoh of ancient Egypt, was buried in a tomb in the Valley of the Kings. Thirty-two centuries later, in AD 1922, his tomb was rediscovered, with all its treasures still intact, by the British archaeologist Howard Carter and his team. Thanks to them, the forgotten pharaoh, Tutankhamun, became world famous. One person is missing from these pages – Harry Burton was a photographer who worked with Howard Carter and took many of the black-and-white pictures used in this book. He was always behind the camera, which is why he does not appear in any of the photographs!

THE CHIEF MINISTER

Tutankhamun's chief minister, Ay, was the most powerful man in Egypt after the king. When Tutankhamun died, Ay became the next pharaoh. By then he was an old man, and he reigned for just four years.

Ay

PRIESTS

The chief priest at a royal funeral was called the *Sem* priest. He wore a leopard skin. Other priests prepared the pharaoh's body for the afterlife and then installed his mummified body in the tomb.

Chief priest

THE YOUNG QUEEN

Tutankhamun was married to his half-sister, Ankhesenamun (see page 42). After Tutankhamun's death, his successor, Ay, married Ankhesenamun to strengthen his own claim to the throne.

Ankhesenamun

ROYAL COUPLE
This vivid picture of the young king and his queen is carved on the golden throne found in the tomb. Ankhesenamun is anointing her husband with perfume.

Tutankhamun

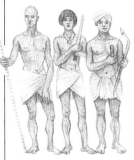

Workers and craftsmen

CRAFTSMEN

Large numbers of workers and craftsmen were needed to cut Tutankhamun's tomb out of the rock. They had to carve and then decorate it. Many of them lived in a special workers' village near the Valley of the Kings, called Deir el-Medina.

Tomb robbers

ROBBERS

Egyptian rulers were buried with great treasures, which attracted tomb robbers. All the tombs in the Valley of the Kings were robbed – even Tutankhamun's tomb was disturbed. Often the robbers were the very workers who had built the tomb.

THE BOY KING

Tutankhamun was probably the son of Akhenaten, the pharaoh whose changes to the religion of Egypt caused turmoil (see page 43). He was only nine when he came to the throne, so the real power was in the hands of his chief minister, Ay, and of the head of the army, Horemheb. Tutankhamun died when he was only 18, and was buried with magnificent treasures.

THE SPONSOR

Lord Carnarvon was a wealthy British aristocrat. He took up archaeology as a hobby after his doctor advised him to spend winters in Egypt to improve his health. Lord Carnarvon sponsored Howard Carter to dig for him in Egypt.

LADY EVELYN

Carnarvon's daughter, Lady Evelyn Herbert, was his "devoted companion in all his Egyptian work".

HIGHCLERE CASTLE

Lord Carnarvon's collection of ancient Egyptian art was kept in his grand house in England.

Lord Carnarvon

Howard Carter

Carter with Callender
When Carter started work in Tutankhamun's tomb, he needed help from other experts. He is pictured here with Arthur Callender (right), who was an engineer and architect.

Mace and Lucas
Arthur Mace (left) was an American archaeologist who helped Carter write the first volume of his book about the tomb. Alfred Lucas (right) was an expert in conserving ancient treasures.

Local workers
Carter hired hundreds of local workers to help him discover the site of Tutankhamun's tomb. They moved thousands of tons of stone debris in the search for the tomb.

THE ARCHAEOLOGIST

At the age of 17, Howard Carter's drawing skills got him a job in Egypt, copying tomb paintings. There his passion for archaeology began. In 1899 he became Inspector General of Monuments, but his real ambition was to lead an archaeological dig in the Valley of the Kings. In 1907 Carter teamed up with Carnarvon, who shared his belief that a great discovery could still be made in the valley.

THE VALLEY OF THE KINGS

ONE OF THE WORLD'S MOST AMAZING burial grounds lies in a desert valley in Egypt, near the modern city of Luxor. For 500 years, the Valley of the Kings was a royal cemetery, where the some of the most famous pharaohs of ancient Egypt were buried, surrounded by treasures, in tombs cut out of the valley cliffs. Modern archaeologists began excavating the valley seriously in 1898, but they did not find a single tomb with its treasures intact. In 1912, Theodore Davis, an American Egyptologist, announced, "The Valley of the Tombs is now exhausted". But Howard Carter believed that at least one tomb was still hidden in the valley – that of the forgotten pharaoh, Tutankhamun.

THE VALLEY IN THE WEST
The ancient Egyptians believed that the land of the dead lay in the west, where the sun set. For this reason, their cemeteries were usually situated on the west bank of the Nile. The Valley of the Kings was particularly suitable as a royal burial ground, because it had narrow entrances that could easily be guarded against tomb robbers.

EYEWITNESS
"The Valley of the Tombs of the Kings – the very name is full of romance."

Howard Carter

MAP OF THE VALLEY
Nearly every pharaoh of the New Kingdom period (1550–1070 BC) was buried in the Valley of the Kings. By 1922, archaeologists had uncovered about 60 tombs and burial pits in the valley. They gave each tomb a number. Many of the tombs are still known by these numbers, because the names of the occupants have not yet been discovered.

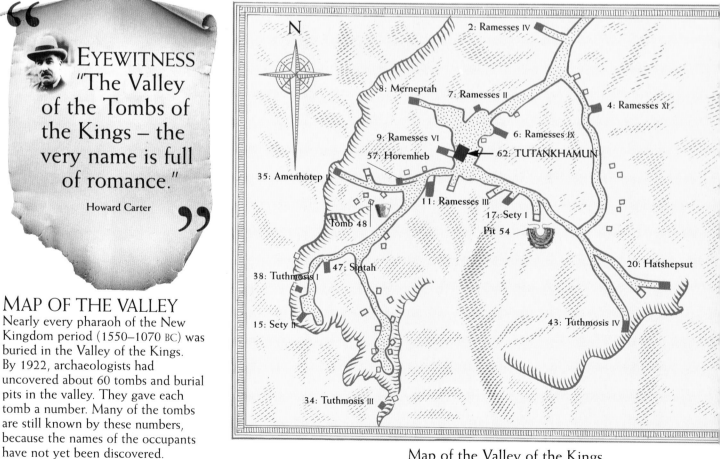

Map of the Valley of the Kings

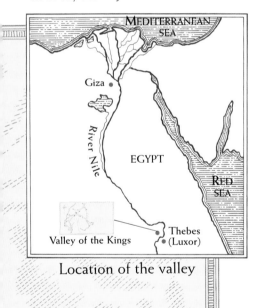

Following the clues

DURING HIS EXCAVATIONS, Davis made two discoveries connected with Tutankhamun. This evidence proved to Carter that Tutankhamun was buried somewhere in the valley.

Faience cup

Collar of flowers

Linen bag

Pottery vessel

Inscribed cup
In 1905, a small faience (pottery) cup inscribed with Tutankhamun's name was found near tomb 48 by Ayrton, one of Davis' team.

Pit 54 artefacts
In 1907, Ayrton found collars and objects used for embalming near pit 54. Tutankhamun's name was on some of these things.

THEODORE DAVIS
Only one team of archaeologists was permitted to work in the valley at a time. From 1902, the permit was held by Davis, a wealthy American who found 35 tombs. When he gave up the permit in 1915, the way was clear for Carter.

The pyramids at Giza
Egypt's early rulers were buried in pyramids. But these huge monuments inevitably attracted tomb robbers. The builders concealed the entrances and the route to the burial chamber, but the pyramids were still robbed. In the hope of defeating the thieves, later kings were buried in hidden tombs in the Valley of the Kings.

Location of the valley

CARTER STARTS WORK
Carter admitted, "Ever since my first visit to Egypt in 1890, it had been my ambition to dig in the Valley". From 1917–22, his army of workmen cleared thousands of tons of sand and rock chippings from the valley floor in a painstaking search for the entrance to Tutankhamun's tomb. But they found nothing. Had Davis been right all along?

Inside a valley tomb
Many of the tombs that had been uncovered in the valley by the 1920s were magnificent. Their walls were decorated with beautiful paintings, like these in the tomb of Ramesses VI (above). But every one of the tombs had been robbed. So far no one had found a tomb containing the treasures that were buried with a pharaoh.

Key to maps

 Edge of the valley

Important royal tombs, with their numbers

Other tombs and burial pits

Tutankhamun's tomb

 Tutankhamun's faience cup found here in 1905

 Tutankhamun's embalming materials found here in 1907

EYEWITNESS

"Hardly had I arrived at work the next morning (4th November) than the unusual silence... made me realize that something out of the ordinary had happened; and I was greeted by the announcement that a step cut into the rock had been discovered."

Howard Carter

The staircase
Large amounts of debris were cleared, and the sunken stairway emerged. At the twelfth step the top of a sealed door appeared. This photograph of the entrance was taken by Harry Burton after the tomb was opened.

THE HIDDEN STEPS

Plan of the tomb

TUTANKHAMUN'S TOMB might well have remained lost for ever. By the summer of 1922, Lord Carnarvon was so disappointed by their lack of success that he told Carter he wanted to pull out. Eventually they agreed to try one last season, excavating a small area near the tomb of Ramesses VI. On 1 November, Carter's workmen began clearing the remains of some ancient huts. Only three days later a stone step was discovered. Was this the entrance to a tomb? Further digging uncovered a stairway, then the top of a blocked doorway covered with ancient seals. But these seals gave no hint of who was buried in the tomb. Containing his excitement, Carter ordered the staircase to be filled in again and sent a telegram to Lord Carnarvon, summoning him to Egypt.

LOCAL WORKERS
The local workmen hired by Carter shared in the rediscovery of Egypt's past. One of the workmen discovered the first stone step and others guarded the staircase until it was temporarily filled in again.

The forgotten tomb

Hidden under another tomb
Only luck had kept Tutankhamun's tomb intact. It was hidden by its surroundings in the Valley of the Kings, and had quickly been forgotten. About 200 years later, Pharaoh Ramesses VI had his own tomb cut out of the rock almost directly above it. Ramesses' workmen built their huts right over the entrance to Tutankamun's tomb. They hid it still further, by burying the site under the chippings of stone that they were digging out of Ramesses' tomb.

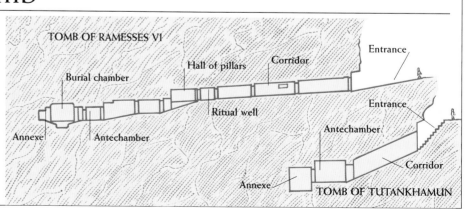

TOMB OF RAMESSES VI
Burial chamber
Hall of pillars
Corridor
Entrance
Ritual well
Annexe
Antechamber
Entrance
Antechamber
Annexe
Corridor
TOMB OF TUTANKHAMUN

UNCOVERING THE STAIRCASE

On 24 November, with Carnarvon eagerly watching, Carter, now joined by his colleague Arthur Callender, dug out the whole staircase. It was slow, laborious work, but eventually 16 steps and an entire doorway were revealed.

BACK-BREAKING WORK
The workmen carried out the stone chippings in wicker baskets.

PUZZLING INSCRIPTIONS
All the debris was carefully sifted. The names of several pharaohs were found carved on fragments of pottery.

KEEPING RECORDS
Carter's skills as an artist proved extremely useful – he made careful drawings of everything they found.

WORRYING EVIDENCE
Carter could now see that the door had been repaired in two places. This was evidence that the tomb had been broken in to in ancient times.

THE VITAL CLUE

When the door was completely uncovered, Carter was finally able to read more of the seals and find a name – Tutankhamun! After years of searching, he had finally found the tomb, but what was inside?

EYEWITNESS
"At last have made a wonderful discovery in the Valley; a magnificent tomb with seals intact; re-covered same for your arrival; congratulations."

Carter's telegram to Lord Carnarvon, 6 November 1922

Carnarvon arrives in Egypt
Carter's telegram brought Carnarvon to Egypt in a hurry. With his daughter, Lady Evelyn Herbert, he arrived in Luxor on 23 November and was met by Carter and an Egyptian official.

The seals

THE ANCIENT EGYPTIANS stamped seals into the wet plaster on tomb doors. The seals showed whose tomb it was and which officials had sealed it.

Jackal and nine captives
This seal was used by the officials who were in charge of the Valley of the Kings. They stamped it on the door of a royal tomb when they closed it for the last time.

Nebkheprure
When he was crowned, a pharaoh was given a series of five names that made up his formal title. This seal shows Tutankhamun's fourth name, Nebkheprure. Seals like this one convinced Carter that this was Tutankhamun's tomb.

BREAKING THROUGH

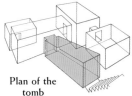

Plan of the tomb

WHAT LAY BEHIND THE SEALED doorway? On 25 November, Carter and his team dug out the rough stones that blocked the door and discovered a downward-sloping corridor, filled from floor to ceiling with limestone chippings. The workmen set to work at once to clear it. Unfortunately, there were signs that someone – probably tomb robbers – had tunnelled through the rubble in ancient times. Worse still, the whole layout reminded Carter of some of his earlier finds, which had turned out to be just stores for objects removed from other tombs. Was this Tutankhamun's tomb after all? After digging for about 9 m (30 ft) they came to a second sealed doorway and broke it open...

HEAD OF TUTANKHAMUN
One encouraging find was this head of Tutankhamun. He is shown as the sun god, Re, emerging from a lotus flower. Months later, the head was discovered, packed to be shipped out of Egypt. Carter said it was waiting to be registered, but was he trying to keep it for himself?

STEPS TO THE OUTSIDE
No machinery could be used to clear the rubble. Each basket of chippings had to be carried up the steps by hand and its contents dumped outside.

LIGHTING THE WAY
There was already an electricity supply to the Valley of the Kings, so only extra wiring and lamps were needed to light the corridor.

AMONG THE CHIPPINGS
Mixed with the chippings, Carter found jars, vases, clay seals, bronze razors, and pieces of jewellery. These objects were probably dropped by the tomb robbers as they made a hasty escape.

THE CORRIDOR
The corridor was about 1.7 m (5 ft 6 in) wide – the same width as the stairs – and 2 m (6 ft 6 in) high. Like the stairs, it was completely filled with stone chippings – probably the material which had been cut out when it was originally excavated.

WORKERS IN LINE
Carter's workmen formed a line to pass out the debris, in just the same way as the ancient Egyptians worked.

CLEARING THE RUBBLE
The team painstakingly sorted and cleared the rubble by hand, so that any object they found could be saved.

Signs of robbery

THE CORRIDOR SHOWED "signs of more than one opening and reclosing of the tomb", Carter noted. He knew this from looking at the filling.

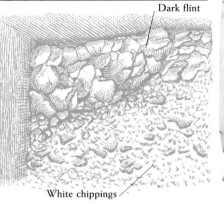

Dark flint

White chippings

The evidence
Most of the filling was white chippings and dust, but the top left-hand corner was filled with dark flint. A tunnel had been dug through this part and then filled in again.

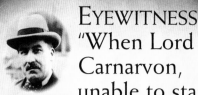

EYEWITNESS
"When Lord Carnarvon, unable to stand the suspense any longer, inquired anxiously, 'Can you see anything?' it was all I could do to get out the words, 'Yes, wonderful things.'"

Howard Carter

TUNNELLING THROUGH
The corridor had only been filled with rubble after the first gang of robbers broke in. The second gang, faced with a corridor full of chippings, tunnelled through just below the ceiling. Carter reckoned it would have taken about eight hours of digging.

CAN YOU SEE ANYTHING?
Lord Carnarvon, Lady Evelyn, and Callender waited anxiously as Carter looked through the hole in the door.

CARTER'S FIRST GLIMPSE
Carter stuck a rod through the second sealed doorway, but felt nothing. There must be a space behind the door. He widened the hole, lit a candle, then peered in. An amazing sight met his eyes.

The candle test
Although they had electric torches, Carter used a candle when he first looked into the tomb. He was carrying out the old-fashioned test for bad air. Inert gases would put the candle out, though flammable gases might explode!

Two tombs revealed
The entrance to Tutankhamun's tomb is behind the low wall in the foreground of this photograph. Cut into the hill behind is the tomb of Ramesses VI, which was built almost on top of Tutankhamun's tomb.

Visitors to the tomb
The news of the discovery soon spread and a crowd of journalists and tourists arrived in the valley. They waited each day by the tomb entrance, hoping to see something exciting.

THE ANTECHAMBER

Plan of the tomb

CARTER WIDENED THE hole in the door, so that both he and Carnarvon could see in, and pushed through an electric torch. Caught in its beam of light and distorted by the shadows, was a sight so extraordinary that at first it was bewildering. Gradually, they made out three gilded couches in the shapes of strange animals, while to the right were two life-sized black statues, clothed in gold. Piled up all around were inlaid caskets, alabaster vases, egg-shaped boxes, and a huge heap of chariot parts. Chipping out an entrance, Carter led Carnarvon, Lady Evelyn, and Callender down into the small room, where they wandered around, examining the treasures. There was no sign of a coffin, but Carter noticed that the two black statues were guarding a sealed doorway. He realized that this was just an outer room, or antechamber, and that the king's real burial place must lie behind the mysterious door.

EYEWITNESS

"At first I could see nothing..., but presently, as my eyes grew accustomed to the light, details of the room within emerged slowly from the mist, strange animals, statues, and gold – everywhere the glint of gold."

Howard Carter

Funeral rites

The evidence
There was evidence in this room of the ceremonies that took place during the king's funeral. Carter found two gilded rattles, called *sistra*, which were used by priestesses. Bouquets of persea and olive leaves had been left as offerings in front of the guardian statues and, amazingly, they were still intact 3,000 years later.

Priestess leaving an offering

IN SEARCH OF TREASURE
The robbers rifled through boxes and chests, looking for small objects that they could sell easily.

REJECTED RICHES
Even though they were covered in gold, large objects like the chariots and couches were of no interest to the robbers. They were just too big to carry.

WRAPPED UP
The robbers took jewellery, oils, cosmetics, ointments, and linen. They wrapped their loot in cloth bundles to make it easy to carry away.

WAR CHARIOT
Horse-drawn chariots are often shown in ancient Egyptian paintings like this one from the side of a box found in the tomb. It shows Tutankhamun leading the Egyptian army against the Syrians. Before 1922, only two complete chariots had ever been found. There were six of them in Tutankhamun's tomb.

Couch

THE FUNERAL

Workers hurriedly filling the antechamber after Tutankhamun's funeral in 1327 BC found the space very cramped. Caskets and boxes had to be piled under and on top of the couches. The chariots had to be taken apart to get them into the tomb so they were stacked in pieces.

GUARDIANS OF THE DEAD

The two guardian statues were life-sized portraits of Tutankhamun. One represented the king, the other his ka, *or spirit.*

Preserving the treasures
Carter and his team had to clear the antechamber before they could explore the other rooms. Each object was numbered, described on a record card, photographed, and then removed for preservation treatment in a nearby tomb used as a "field laboratory".

THE ROBBERIES

Only a few years after the funeral, in about 1323 BC, tomb robbers looted the tomb. They worked fast, breaking open containers and passing objects out through a hole in the door. The tomb was robbed at least twice. The first gang of robbers probably got away safely, but the second gang may not have been so lucky.

A QUICK GET-AWAY

Other robbers waited in the corridor to receive the objects as they were passed out.

A robber's fate

Riches or death
Robbers could get rich by selling their loot, but if they were caught, they faced a terrible punishment. First they were tortured by having the soles of their feet beaten with rods. Then they suffered an agonising death impaled on a sharpened wooden stake.

Sealed door

THE DISCOVERY

After the robberies, the antechamber stood undisturbed for more than 3,000 years until 1922, when Carter and his team came in. They were amazed by the quantity of treasures piled up in the room, many of them flashing with gold. These objects were all part of the equipment that the ancient Egyptians believed a pharaoh would need in the afterlife.

Chariot wheels

Doorway to corridor

Chariot body

THE BURIAL CHAMBER

CARTER COULD FEEL

the audience's excitement as he dismantled the sealed door leading from the antechamber. Slowly he revealed what, at first, looked like "a solid wall of gold". On 17 February 1923, after seven weeks spent clearing the antechamber, the formal opening of the door was taking place before a specially invited audience. As he scrambled through the hole in the doorway and into the small room beyond, Carter discovered that the "wall of gold" was in fact one side of a gilded shrine, so huge that it almost filled the room. He realized that he was inside the king's burial chamber. This was the first of four shrines, fitted one inside another, with a great carved sarcophagus (stone coffin) at the centre. Inside that were three coffins, again one inside the other. In the last coffin, wearing a mask of beaten gold, lay the mummy of Tutankhamun.

Plan of the tomb

PULLEY SYSTEM
Carter had to use a system of wires and pulleys to raise the lid of the sarcophagus and then lift out the coffins, because they were so heavy. Here the second coffin is being slowly lifted out of the outermost coffin.

MUMMY AND MASK
The mummy wore a gold mask – a portrait of Tutankhamun.

THIRD COFFIN
The innermost coffin was made of beaten gold.

SECOND COFFIN
The second coffin was gilded wood with coloured glass inlays.

FIRST COFFIN
The outermost coffin was made from gilded cypress wood.

SARCOPHAGUS
Tutankhamun's sarcophagus was carved from a huge block of quartzite stone.

Goddess Isis

FOURTH SHRINE
The innermost shrine was covered with carvings of gods and goddesses. Isis and Nephthys guarded the doors, while the sky goddess Nut and hawk-headed Horus looked down from the ceiling.

Religious inscriptions

THIRD SHRINE
Like all the others, the third shrine was gilded and inscribed with extracts from religious writings. These included spells from the *Book of the Dead* to help Tutankhamun find his way through the dangers of the underworld.

Linen pall

Frame

SECOND SHRINE
A linen pall (burial cloth) hung over a rough framework between the first and second shrines. The doors of the second shrine were still sealed, so Carter knew that the tomb robbers had not reached the king's mummy.

FIRST SHRINE

The outermost shrine was made of cedarwood, gilded and inlaid with blue faience (glazed pottery). It was decorated with protective symbols, such as *wedjat* eyes and *djed* pillars (see page 39). The seals on the doors of this shrine had been broken by the tomb robbers.

TO THE TREASURY
On the east side of the chamber lay an open doorway leading to a smaller room, full of treasures. Carter named the room the treasury.

Ka

Osiris   Tutankhamun

WALL PAINTINGS

The burial chamber was the only room in the tomb with decorated walls. The wall paintings showed a sequence of scenes from Tutankhamun's funeral and his arrival in the underworld. Here, the dead king is entering the underworld, followed by his *ka* (spirit), and welcomed by the god Osiris.

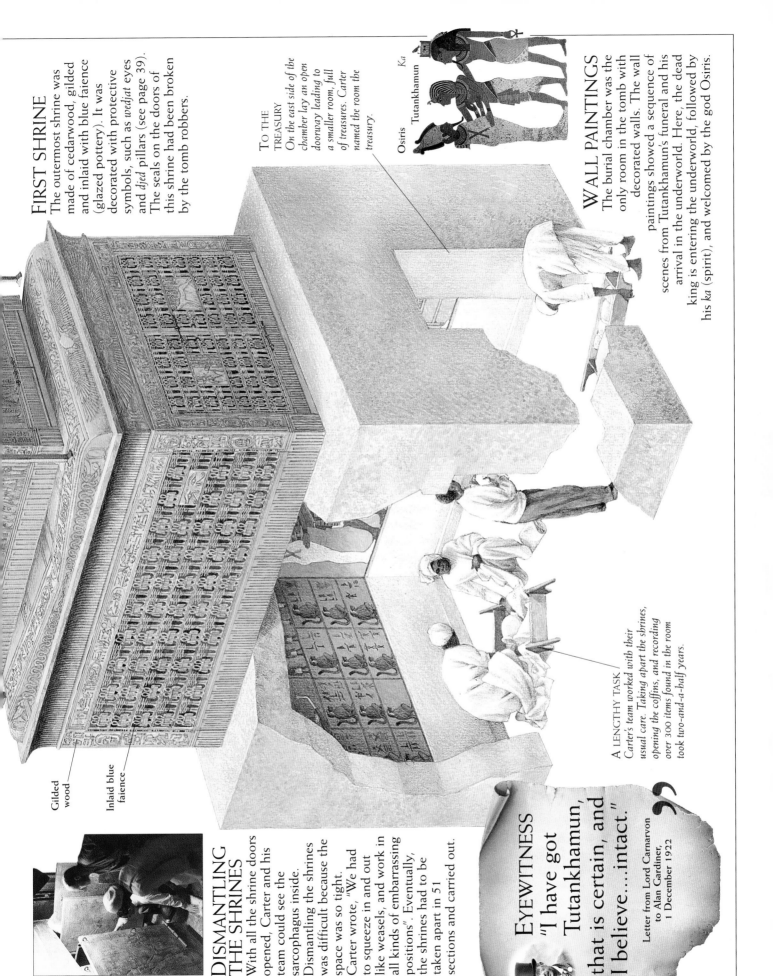

Gilded wood

Inlaid blue faience

A LENGTHY TASK
Carter's team worked with their usual care. Taking apart the shrines, opening the coffins, and recording over 300 items found in the room took two-and-a-half years.

DISMANTLING THE SHRINES

With all the shrine doors opened, Carter and his team could see the sarcophagus inside. Dismantling the shrines was difficult because the space was so tight. Carter wrote, "We had to squeeze in and out like weasels, and work in all kinds of embarrassing positions". Eventually, the shrines had to be taken apart in 51 sections and carried out.

EYEWITNESS
"I have got Tutankhamun, that is certain, and I believe....intact."

Letter from Lord Carnarvon to Alan Gardiner, 1 December 1922

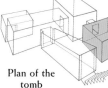

Plan of the tomb

THE TREASURY

Statue of Anubis

BEYOND THE BURIAL CHAMBER, THROUGH an open doorway, lay a smaller room that Carter called the treasury. Inside were more wonders. A dramatic statue of Anubis, the jackal-headed god of mummification, crouched in the doorway, guarding the room. On the far side stood a huge gilded shrine, protected by the figures of four goddesses. According to Arthur Mace, it was "the most beautiful object I have seen anywhere". All around lay caskets, shrines, and chests, containing jewellery, amulets, magical objects, and gold statuettes of the gods and of Tutankhamun himself. There were even several model boats, with their sails and rigging still intact. It was all so extraordinary that Carter had to block the doorway so that he wouldn't be distracted while he was working in the burial chamber.

AT WORK
The treasury presented Carter and his team with another difficult task. Over 500 objects had to be removed, catalogued, and preserved. The robbers had reached the treasury too. They had stolen jewellery and gold figures, but had not disturbed much.

SHRINES
Each of these small wooden shrines contained several gilded figures of Tutankhamun.

Assembly of the shrine

THE CANOPIC SHRINE contained the king's liver, lungs, stomach, and intestines. These organs were removed from the body to stop them rotting inside the mummy.

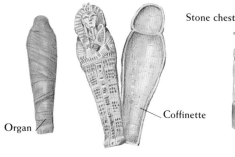

Organ

Coffinette

Stone chest

Stopper

Lid of chest

1 Each of the four organs was embalmed, wrapped in linen, and then put in a coffinette (small coffin) made of beaten gold.

2 Four hollows were drilled out of the middle of a decorated stone chest. The coffinettes were placed inside these hollows, which formed the canopic jars.

3 Each jar was sealed with a stopper, carved in the shape of the king's head. The facial features were painted in black and the lips were reddened.

Most of these boxes had been looted by the tomb robbers.

CANOPIC SHRINE

Before a body was mummified, certain internal organs were removed and stored in special containers, called canopic jars. This huge shrine was built to contain the king's canopic jars. At its four sides stood statues of the goddesses Isis, Nephthys, Neith, and Selkis.

Canopic shrine

MODEL BOATS
There were 16 models of boats for the king to use in the afterlife. Some were for sailing across the heavens, others for river travel.

Many of the boxes contained a docket – a list of the original contents.

The complete shrine was 2 m (6 ft 6 in) high and 1.2 m (4 ft) wide.

Servants for the afterlife
The ancient Egyptians believed that in the afterlife the dead king might be asked to perform hard tasks, such as working in the fields. To avoid this, he was buried with *shabti* figures – servants who would do the work for him. Tutankhamun had one *shabti* for each day of the year.

Tutankhamun's children?
A plain wooden box found in the treasury contained two tiny coffins. Each held a mummified foetus. Professor Derry, who examined the king's mummy in 1925, found that these were the bodies of two stillborn baby girls. They were probably the children of Tutankhamun and his wife, Ankhesenamun.

Cornice

Linen shroud

Gilded sled

Shrine

4 The chest was tied with cords to two sleds, both made of wood covered in gilded plaster. A dark linen shroud was laid over the chest.

5 Finally, a gilded wooden shrine was placed over the chest, topped by a cornice. The completed shrine was protected by statues of four goddesses.

THE ANNEXE

Plan of the tomb

WHEN CARTER FIRST looked round the antechamber, he spotted a sealed door behind one of the couches. He climbed through a small hole in this door at ground level, and discovered a room beyond – the annexe. This was the last room to be cleared – it was not until October 1927 that Carter and his team could begin work there. Although it was the smallest room in the tomb, the annexe was crammed with an extraordinary jumble of objects, "tumbled any way one upon the other", wrote Carter. Things were stacked up nearly 2 m (6 ft) high in places, and there was no space left on the floor. Clearing this room was going to be extremely difficult!

In a rope sling

HE COULD NOT STAND on the floor, so Carter had to start work by leaning into the annexe from the antechamber, suspended in a rope sling.

Rope sling, held up by other members of the team

CLEARING THE ANNEXE

First, Carter and his team had to clear enough space to be able to stand on the annexe floor. Then, as the items were carefully removed, one by one, they used wooden props to stop the remaining heaps of objects from collapsing.

Everything had to be photographed, numbered, and recorded before it was moved.

The floor was covered with baskets, boxes, and jars.

The robbers' hole was under this couch.

Entrance to the annexe
Carter believed that the mess in the annexe had been caused by the tomb robbers. They had broken in from the antechamber, through a small hole in the wall. The officials who repaired the rest of the tomb, after the robberies, had not blocked up this hole or tidied the annexe.

IN THE JUMBLE
Scattered around the room were items including an alabaster boat, figures of a lion and a goat, a fan, a sandal, and even a glove.

PASSING THINGS OUT
The floor of the annexe was about 1 m (3 ft) lower than that of the antechamber. This meant that each object had to be lifted out by hand.

Robber's footprint

A THIEF LEAVES HIS MARK

There was probably only enough space for one robber to climb into the annexe. He had searched hurriedly, tipping out boxes, pushing objects aside, or throwing them out of his way. Carter wrote about the robber, "He had done his work just about as thoroughly as an earthquake". The thief had clambered over a white box, and his dirty footprints were still there, over 3,000 years later.

Pots and boxes had been tossed aside in the confusion.

FACT file

The annexe contained a huge variety of objects. Here are just some of the things that were found there:

• 236 shabti figures (see page 21)

• Bows, arrows, throwing sticks, armour, and shields

• Three ordinary beds and a folding "camp-bed"

• Boards and pieces for playing an ancient Egyptian game, called "senet"

• A throne and footstool

• 116 baskets of food and 30 jars of wine

• Cosmetics and a razor

WOODEN PROPS
Big items were held in position with wooden props while other objects were removed.

THE KING'S BEDS
Four beds were found in the annexe. They each had a wooden frame and a woven mattress made of linen or string.

WOODEN STOOL
This wooden stool was painted white and had a curved seat designed to hold a cushion in place.

Grapes · Leeks · Pomegranate · Wild honey · Nuts · Duck

Food
This was the sort of food the ancient Egyptians ate. The dead king would need to eat in the afterlife, so a supply of food was stored in the annexe. This included bread, meats, jars of honey, dates, and dried grapes.

STOREROOM
The annexe was only 4.4 m (14 ft 3 in) long and 2.6 m (8 ft 6 in) wide, but it contained over 2,000 objects. It was intended as a storeroom for oils, ointments, food, and wine. Haste and lack of space meant it was also used to store objects like the beds and chairs, which should have gone in the antechamber or treasury.

Death of Lord Carnarvon

SADLY, LORD CARNARVON did not live to see more than the first stages of the work in the tomb. In February 1923, he cut a mosquito bite on his face while shaving. The bite became infected and Carnarvon collapsed with a fever. He had never been very healthy, and he died of pneumonia on 5 April. Ominously, two weeks earlier, the writer Marie Corelli had warned that punishment would descend on anyone who violated Tutankhamun's tomb.

Carnarvon's death certificate

Carnarvon's razor

The curse
In no time, newspapers invented the story of the "pharaoh's curse", which would bring death to anyone entering the tomb. A few people who had visited the site or were connected with the excavation team did die shortly afterwards. But most did not! Carter himself died in 1939, at the age of 65.

VICTIM OF THE CURSE?
Jay Gould was one of the supposed victims of the curse. He was an American businessman who had made an immense fortune from the railways. Gould caught a cold while visiting the tomb and later died of pneumonia.

UNWRAPPING THE MUMMY

ON 11 NOVEMBER 1925, THREE years after the discovery of the tomb, experts began a post mortem on a 3,000-year-old corpse. Douglas Derry, professor of anatomy from the Egyptian University, had to work carefully, because Tutankhamun's mummy was very fragile. The wrappings had decayed and the mummy was glued so firmly to the coffin that it took four days to get it out. The gold death mask was stuck to the head and had to be removed using hot knives. Only then was the face of the boy-king revealed at last.

KEEPING RECORDS
Burton photographed each stage of the delicate work and Carter made detailed drawings.

The head had been shaved.

An embalmer's cut ran from navel to hip.

The legs had thinned and shrunk.

The body
In this photograph, taken by Harry Burton, Tutankhamun's unwrapped body is lying on a tray of sand, in the position it had been placed in the coffin. The body was in poor condition compared to other royal mummies. The skin was badly preserved – it was brittle and grey.

THE FIRST CUT
Derry cut through the outer shroud to peel back the wrappings. He found many pieces of jewellery under the bandages.

DISAPPOINTMENT
Carter anxiously watched the procedure, disappointed at the state of the mummy.

DERRY AT WORK
Derry could not save the wrappings, and he had to take the body apart to get it out of the coffin and then reassemble it. Unwrapping the head needed extra care – he used a fine, soft brush for the last stages.

MUMMY'S FACE
The mummy's face had cracked, darkened skin and the nose had been flattened by the bandages.

REAL LIFE?
The death mask showed the king as a handsome young man. He may have looked like this in real life.

THE EVIDENCE

Although the body was badly damaged, the team was still able to learn a lot from the post mortem. It showed that Tutankhamun had been a slim young man, 1.65 m (5 ft 5 in) tall. His bones and wisdom teeth indicated that he was about 18 years old when he died. Derry was unable to suggest the cause of death, but a second post mortem, held in 1968, uncovered some dramatic new evidence (see page 43).

Jewellery
More than 150 pieces of jewellery were found on the mummy, placed according to instructions in the *Book of the Dead* (see page 18). This pectoral (chest) ornament is decorated with a sacred scarab beetle.

The coffins

WHEN THEY SAW Tutankhamun's first golden coffin, Carter's team gasped with astonishment. There were in fact three coffins, placed one inside the other.

A resin-based ointment had been poured over the mummy and coffins as part of the mummification process, and had stuck them firmly together.

Nemes head cloth (see page 41)

The crook and flail symbolized divine rule.

Above the face stood the cobra and vulture – goddesses of Lower and Upper Egypt.

The first coffin
The outermost coffin was 2.2 m (7 ft 4 in) long. It was made of wood covered with plaster and gold leaf, and decorated with a *rishi* (feather) pattern.

The second coffin
This coffin, also made of gilded wood, was more elaborate than the first. It was inlaid with red and turquoise glass, and blue pottery.

The third coffin
When the third coffin was finally revealed, the team were amazed to discover that it weighed 110 kg (296 lb), and was made of solid gold.

Full length
This type of coffin is called "mummiform" because it is mummy-shaped. For the ancient Egyptians, the coffin was a house for the dead person's spirit.

Crook and flail

False beard

Vulture and cobra

Treasures of the Tomb

The goddess Isis spreads her wings to protect the dead pharaoh.

THE FOUR ROOMS of Tutankhamun's tomb were crammed with hundreds of objects. These treasures had been carried to the tomb on the day of the king's funeral and were stored there for him to use in the afterlife.

EYEWITNESS

"Let the reader imagine how the objects appeared to us as we looked down upon them from our spy-hole in the blocked doorway, casting the beam of light from our torch – the first light that had pierced the darkness of the chamber for three thousand years – from one group of objects to another, in a vain attempt to interpret the treasure that lay before us...We had never dreamed of anything like this, a roomful – a whole museumful, it seemed – of objects, some familiar, but some the like of which we had never seen, piled one upon another in seemingly endless profusion."

Howard Carter

The inside of one of the doors to the third shrine. The winged figure is the goddess Isis.

STATUETTE OF TUTANKHAMUN

Tutankhamun is wearing the red crown of Lower Egypt (see page 41).

Rafts, like the one he is standing on, were made of reeds and used on the Nile.

In Egyptian mythology, Horus, the son of Osiris, fought and finally killed the evil god Seth, his father's slayer. This gilded statuette shows Tutankhamun as Horus about to spear Seth, who had taken the form of a hippopotamus.

"WONDERFUL THINGS"

FOR AN EGYPTIAN PHARAOH, DEATH was just an unfortunate crossing point between two lives. Beyond death, Tutankhamun's life and his position as pharaoh would continue, so his tomb was filled with the sorts of items a pharaoh would need in his afterlife. These "wonderful things", as Howard Carter described them, included thrones, jewellery, and other symbols of his wealth, as well as practical items, such as furniture, clothes, and food. Many of the items were decorated with images of the king performing important acts, because the Egyptians believed that whatever they showed him doing would become real in the afterlife.

PAINTED BOX

The sides and lid of this box are covered with intricate paintings of the king hunting and at war. Like most of the boxes in the tomb, its contents had been plundered by the robbers.

ANUBIS

The ears and collar are covered in gold.

Guarding the treasury was this black statue of Anubis, the god of mummification and the guardian of the dead. He is sitting on a gilded shrine, which contained items used for mummification.

Gilded shrine

Sled with carrying poles

The shrine is only 50 cm (1 ft 7 in) high and 26 cm (10 in) wide.

LITTLE GOLDEN SHRINE

This tiny wooden shrine is covered in embossed sheets of gold, that show Queen Ankhesenamun lovingly helping the king – as she would in the afterlife. The robbers had stolen a statuette from inside the shrine.

FACT file

- One of the most unusual treasures is a lock of hair from Tutankhamun's grandmother, Queen Tiye.
- The gold in the death mask is worth about £64,000 (US $105,500) at today's gold prices.
- Wrapping up the treasures from the antechamber alone, took 1.6 km (1 mile) of cotton wadding.
- People thought that clearing the tomb would take months. In fact, there were so many treasures that it took Carter's team 10 years.

THE THRONE

This magnificent golden throne was found in the antechamber, hidden under one of the animal couches. The back panel shows the king and queen beneath the rays of the Aten – the sun disc worshipped by Tutankamun's father, Akhenaten.

Aten

The throne is covered in gold and silver, inlaid with coloured glass and semi-precious stones.

The legs are shaped like of those of a lion, and topped with lions' heads to turn away evil.

MODEL BOAT

Sacred boats carried the gods on their journeys, and the dead pharaoh would need boats too. He would use them for activities such as following the voyage of the sun and hunting in the Nile marshes.

ITEMS OF JEWELLERY

The king wore jewellery in life, so naturally he was supplied with plenty of it to wear in the afterlife. There were more than 200 pieces of jewellery in Tutankhamun's tomb, even after the robbers had stolen a large number of the most valuable items.

Winged scarab beetle

These two pieces of jewellery are pectoral (chest) ornaments.

Wedjat eye

PROTECTIVE SPELL
On the back of the mask is a spell which asks various gods to protect each facial feature.

THE DEATH MASK

Probably the most famous item from the tomb is Tutankhamun's death mask, which was found covering the face of his mummy. It is made from two sheets of gold, joined together by hammering, and inlaid with coloured glass, carnelian, and lapis lazuli. The mask weighs about 10 kg (22 lb) and probably shows an idealized image of Tutankhamun's face.

Life & Times
of Tutankhamun

B Y TUTANKHAMUN'S TIME, the kingdom of Egypt had already existed for 1,600 years. It was a stable and prosperous country, whose power and influence stretched far into Africa and Asia. All Egypt's wealth came from farming the rich land watered by the River Nile.

Scribes carefully recorded the amount of grain harvested.

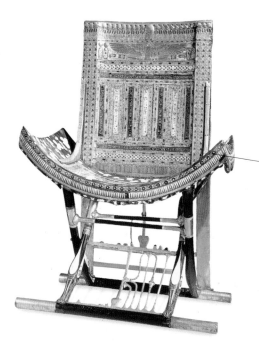

Finely crafted throne, found in Tutankhamun's tomb

Threshed corn was tossed into the air with wooden fans to separate the grain from the chaff.

Corn was trampled by oxen to thresh it.

A wall painting from the tomb of Mennah, scribe to pharaoh Tuthmoses IV, shows farmers at harvest time.

THE KINGDOM OF THE NILE

ANCIENT EGYPT WAS A COUNTRY CLINGING to the banks of a river. Nine-tenths of the country was uninhabitable desert – the Egyptians called it *Deshret*, the "red land". But the final tenth, along the banks of the river Nile, was *Kemet*, the "black land", named after the rich, dark soil where the farmers grew their crops. Most people lived in this region and all the cities were built here. Egypt was a rich and powerful country, ruled by god-kings called pharaohs. Their strong government brought peace and stability – the Egyptian civilization lasted for more than 3,000 years, and the way of life hardly changed in all that time.

THE TWO LANDS

Egypt was traditionally divided into two parts, called the Two Lands. Lower Egypt was the delta region – the wet, marshy area around the many branches of the Nile where it joins the sea. Upper Egypt stretched south in a narrow valley along the banks of the Nile. It was surrounded by desert on both sides, and was much drier than the delta region.

Even today, only a thin strip of land along the Nile can be farmed.

THE RIVER NILE

Each summer, the Nile flooded the land along its banks. It left behind a layer of rich silt, which fertilized the soil. Farmers used a network of canals, dykes, and reservoirs to trap the flood water and channel it on to the land to grow crops. The Nile was also a highway, linking Egypt's cities by cheap boat transport.

Separating the grain from the chaff at harvest time

FARMING

The Egyptians produced far more food than they needed, and were able to sell the excess abroad. Their main crops were wheat and barley. They also grew onions, beans, lentils, many other vegetables, and a range of fruits.

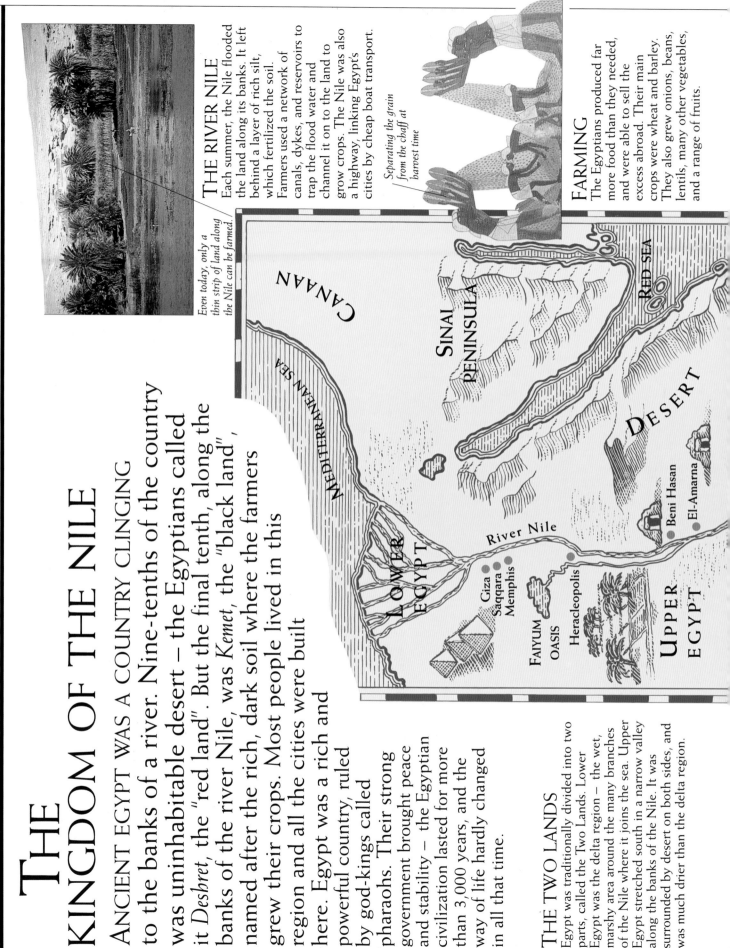

MEDITERRANEAN SEA

CANAAN

SINAI PENINSULA

RED SEA

DESERT

River Nile

LOWER EGYPT

• Giza
• Saqqara
• Memphis

Heracleopolis

FAIYUM OASIS

UPPER EGYPT

• Beni Hasan
• El-Amarna

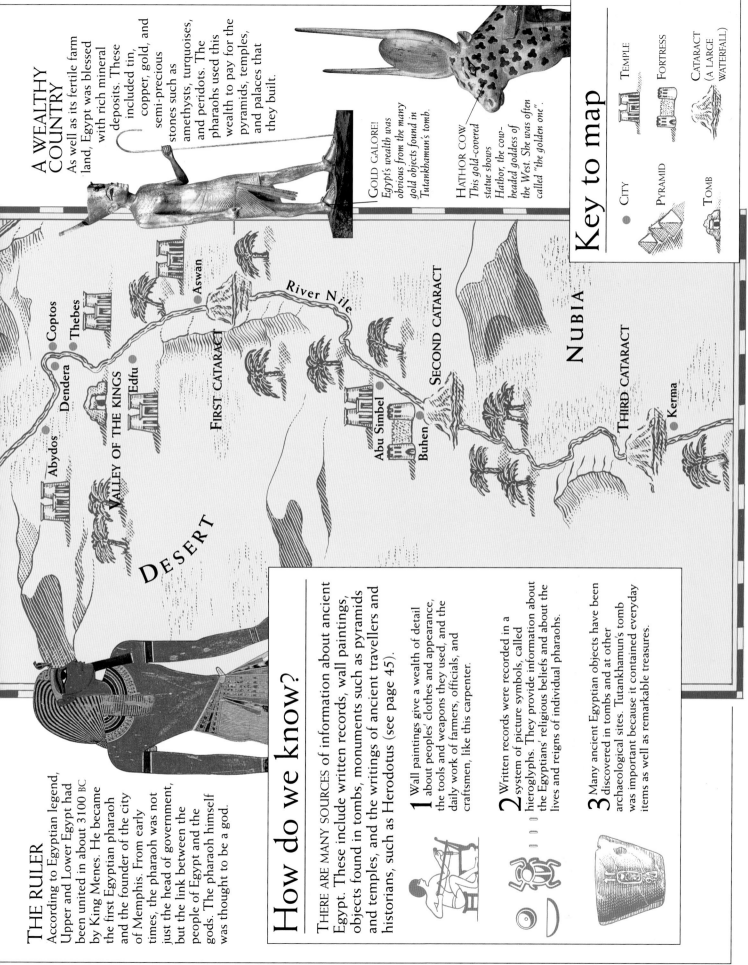

A WEALTHY COUNTRY

As well as its fertile farm land, Egypt was blessed with rich mineral deposits. These included tin, copper, gold, and semi-precious stones such as amethysts, turquoises, and peridots. The pharaohs used this wealth to pay for the pyramids, temples, and palaces that they built.

GOLD GALORE! *Egypt's wealth was obvious from the many gold objects found in Tutankhamun's tomb.*

HATHOR COW *This gold-covered statue shows Hathor, the cow-headed goddess of the West. She was often called "the golden one".*

Key to map

- ● CITY
- 🏛 TEMPLE
- 🏛 FORTRESS
- 🔺 PYRAMID
- ⛰ CATARACT (A LARGE WATERFALL)
- ⛩ TOMB

Coptos
Thebes
Aswan
Dendera
Abydos
Edfu
VALLEY OF THE KINGS
FIRST CATARACT
River Nile
Abu Simbel
Buhen
SECOND CATARACT
THIRD CATARACT
Kerma
NUBIA
DESERT

THE RULER

According to Egyptian legend, Upper and Lower Egypt had been united in about 3100 BC by King Menes. He became the first Egyptian pharaoh and the founder of the city of Memphis. From early times, the pharaoh was not just the head of government, but the link between the people of Egypt and the gods. The pharaoh himself was thought to be a god.

How do we know?

THERE ARE MANY SOURCES of information about ancient Egypt. These include written records, wall paintings, objects found in tombs, monuments such as pyramids and temples, and the writings of ancient travellers and historians, such as Herodotus (see page 45).

1 Wall paintings give a wealth of detail about peoples' clothes and appearance, the tools and weapons they used, and the daily work of farmers, officials, and craftsmen, like this carpenter.

2 Written records were recorded in a system of picture symbols, called hieroglyphs. They provide information about the Egyptians' religious beliefs and about the lives and reigns of individual pharaohs.

3 Many ancient Egyptian objects have been discovered in tombs and at other archaeological sites. Tutankhamun's tomb was important because it contained everyday items as well as remarkable treasures.

GODS AND RELIGION

THE ANCIENT EGYPTIANS WORSHIPPED many gods. At the centre of their beliefs lay the sun god, Re, who could appear in many different forms and had several names. Some gods were shown with a human body and an animal head – the animal that represented their power. For example, Horus, the god of kingship, was represented by a falcon. Some of the most important gods were linked to burial and the afterlife.

AMUN
Amun was the king of the gods. He was often linked to the sun god and was also known as Amun-Re. His nature was secret – Amun means "'hidden".

OSIRIS
Osiris was murdered by his brother, Seth. His wife, Isis, brought him back to life and he became the god of the underworld. Osiris represented both the rebirth of the land through the Nile floods, and the rebirth of the body in the afterlife.

Isis with her wings outstretched

ISIS
Isis was a powerful mother goddess and protector. She brought Osiris back from the dead and then cared for their son, Horus. When Isis searched for the body of Osiris, she took the form of a bird called a kite, so she was often shown with wings.

THE JOURNEY TO THE AFTERLIFE
The crossing to the afterlife was full of perils. The dead person had to know what to expect and have magic spells ready to ward off the many dangers. The dead soul wandered the underworld, looking for the Hall of Judgement, where their past life would be judged by the god Osiris.

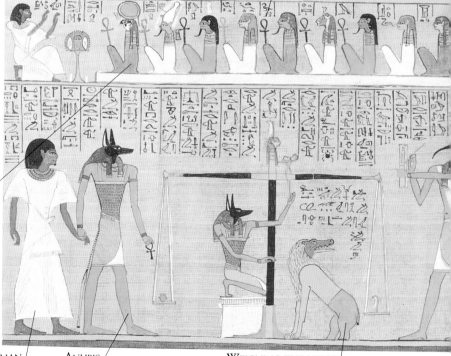

BOOK OF THE DEAD
This Hall of Judgement picture comes from the tomb of Hunefer, a scribe who died in about 1285 BC.

Gods from each of Egypt's districts questioned the dead man about his life.

THE DEAD MAN
The dead man was led into the Hall of Judgement by the jackal-headed god, Anubis.

ANUBIS
Real jackals often roamed the graveyards of Egypt, so Anubis was linked to the dead. He was the god of embalming and guardian of the dead.

WEIGHING THE HEART
After the dead man had been questioned, Anubis weighed his heart against the feather of truth. If he had lied, his heart was eaten by the Devourer of the Dead and he would not enter the afterlife.

THE GODS' HOMES

Karnak, Luxor, and the other great temples were built as homes for the gods. The sacred statue of the god was kept in the innermost sanctuary of the temple. Each day, the pharaoh or the high priest carried out religious ceremonies and offered the statue food and drink. On festival days, the statue was paraded outside the temple, so that ordinary people could consult the god.

Symbols of the gods

THE EGYPTIANS BELIEVED that certain symbols were able to protect against evil or bring good luck. Some of these symbols were linked to specific gods, and could summon the gods' special powers.

Wedjat **eye**
The *wedjat* eye represented the eye of Horus. He had lost the eye in a fight with evil, but it was magically restored. The eye was used to protect mummies and ward off evil.

Djed **pillar**
The symbol of the god Osiris was the *djed* pillar. It represented survival, stability, and the possibility of rebirth in the afterlife. The word *djed* means "stability".

Girdle of Isis
The protective power of the goddess Isis was called up by the *tyet* symbol, which is also known as the Girdle of Isis. The *tyet* was probably an image of a knot of cloth.

LIFE AFTER DEATH

A painting from the tomb of Sennedjem in Western Thebes shows what the Egyptians expected in the afterlife – a happier version of their earthly life. The dead man and his wife are ploughing and reaping in the "field of reeds", a realm of the afterlife situated at the northern edge of the sky.

Becoming an Osiris
The magical rebirth of Osiris gave the Egyptians hope that they too could "become an Osiris" and live for ever in the afterlife. To achieve this, a dead person had to imitate Osiris in every way. Tutankhamun's mummy was prepared with the arms crossed and holding the crook and flail, to make him look like Osiris.

Osiris \ Tutankhamun

Osiris bed
Egyptian tombs sometimes contained an Osiris bed. This was a wooden frame in the shape of the god, filled with Nile soil, and planted with corn seeds. The seeds would germinate in the tomb, symbolizing the rebirth of Osiris and that of the dead person.

This Osiris bed was found in the treasury of Tutankhamun's tomb, still filled with dried-out germinated corn.

HORUS
If the dead man had told the truth and led a good life, Horus, the falcon-headed god of kingship, presented him to Osiris.

OSIRIS
Osiris welcomed the dead man, who would now "become an Osiris" himself and live for ever in the kingdom of the dead.

ISIS AND NEPHTHYS
Osiris was attended by his wife, Isis, and her sister, Nephthys, who watched the judgement.

THE PHARAOH

FACT file

When a Pharaoh was crowned, he was given a series of five names that made up his formal title. These are Tutankhamun's names and titles:

● The Horus name:
Ka-nakht tut-mesut
(Strong bull, best of all created beings)

● The "He of the Two Ladies" name:
Nefer-hepu segereh-tawy sehetep-netjeru nebu
(Perfect law-maker, who calms the Two Lands and makes the gods content)

● The golden falcon name:
Wetjes-khau sehetep netjeru
(He who displays the regalia, and makes the gods content)

● The prenomen: *Nebkheprure*
(The lordly appearance of the god Re)

● The nomen: *Tutankhamun*
(The living image of the god Amun)

LIKE ALL THE PHARAOHS OF ANCIENT Egypt, Tutankhamun was worshipped as a living god. The pharaoh had immense power and wealth, and great responsibilities. He made offerings to gain the gods' favour for Egypt, he performed ceremonies to ensure that the land would be fertile, and he had a duty to build monuments which would please the gods. He made all the laws, and was also commander-in-chief of the army. Above all, the pharaoh had to maintain *ma'at* (harmony and order) and hold the regions of Upper and Lower Egypt together. One of his many titles was the "Lord of the Two Lands".

HOLDING COURT
Tutankhamun would have held court seated beneath a canopy on his golden throne (see page 33) and holding the crook and flail.

Fan bearer

Ay

MINISTERS IN ATTENDANCE
Tutankhamun would have been attended by servants and supported by his officials, especially Ay, the chief minister.

Scribes carefully recorded all the king's pronouncements.

LEADING THE ARMY

Pharaohs were trained as warriors and traditionally led Egypt's armies in battle. On a box from his tomb, Tutankhamun is shown defeating the Syrians and Nubians, but there is no evidence that he ever fought in real life.

RIDING ALONE
The pharaoh is often shown fighting from a chariot, at the head of the army.

HEAD OF GOVERNMENT

The pharaoh made all the laws, set the level of taxes, and decided on Egypt's foreign policy. In theory, he personally supervised all the affairs of state, but in practice he had a host of officials to carry out his instructions.

Pharaoh's regalia

Nekhbet, vulture goddess of Upper Egypt

Wadjit, cobra goddess of Lower Egypt

STATUES, PAINTINGS, AND CARVINGS show that the pharaoh wore special clothing and carried regalia (symbols of royalty) to show his status as a divine king.

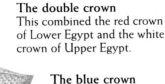

The double crown
This combined the red crown of Lower Egypt and the white crown of Upper Egypt.

The blue crown
The blue crown was linked to the sun god and was worn by New Kingdom pharaohs.

The gods had beards, so the pharaoh wore a false one.

The *nemes* cloth
The pharaoh's distinctive striped headdress was called the *nemes* cloth.

Crook

Flail

The crook and flail
The shepherd's crook and corn-beating flail were emblems of the god Osiris and important parts of the regalia.

The Queen
A pharaoh often had several wives, but only one of them was Queen. Like many other pharaohs, Tutankhamun married his sister. Pharaohs may have done this to strengthen their claim to the throne, or to imitate the gods, who were often married to their sisters.

Ministers and officials
In addition to a chief minister, a pharaoh appointed two officials called viziers to rule Upper and Lower Egypt. Other officials supervized the treasury, the granaries, and the construction of temples and palaces.

Nine bows symbolize Egypt's enemies

Two bound captives

OPENING THE DYKES
This ceremony took place after the Nile flood had subsided. Traditionally, the pharaoh cut the first irrigation channel.

RELIGIOUS DUTIES
The pharaoh was Egypt's religious leader and had many duties, such as making offerings to the gods in their temples. He also used his divine powers in ceremonies to bring the annual Nile floods and water the land for crops.

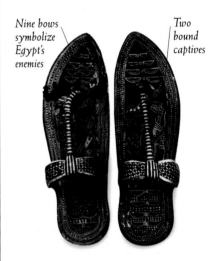

Decorated sandals
The pharaoh had a duty to defeat Egypt's enemies. Many paintings show him victorious in battle. Tutankhamun's sandals have pictures of Syrian and Nubian captives on the soles. As he walked, these enemies would be crushed underfoot.

BUILDING A TOMB
A pharaoh began to prepare his tomb early in his reign, because it took years to build. Tutankhamun died young, and his tomb was unfinished. He was hurriedly buried in someone else's tomb.

WHO WAS TUTANKHAMUN?

"WHAT DO WE REALLY know about this Tutankhamun?" wrote Carter. "Remarkably little.... The one outstanding feature of his life was that he died and was buried." We know so little about Tutankamun's life that experts are not even certain who he was. This is partly because the Egyptians themselves tried to wipe out all records of Tutankhamun because he was related to Akhenaten, the pharaoh who fell out of favour. Discovering the facts about the real Tutankhamun, 3,000 years later, is like trying to make sense of a jigsaw puzzle with many pieces missing.

FAMILY TREE

Experts still disagree about who Tutankhamun was. Some think he was Akhenaten's son, others think he was Akhenaten's brother. And no one knows who Smenkhkare was. This seems to be the most likely version of the family tree.

KEY
m = married
1390–1352 = dates of pharaoh's reign

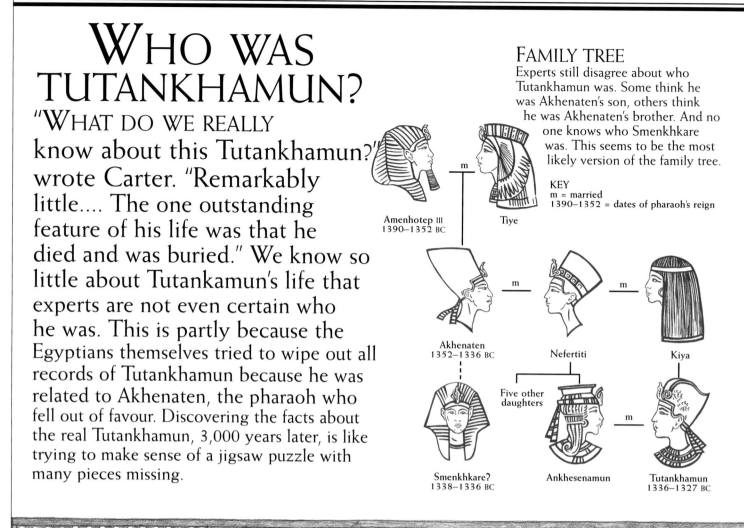

Amenhotep III
1390–1352 BC

Tiye

Akhenaten
1352–1336 BC

Nefertiti

Kiya

Smenkhkare?
1338–1336 BC

Five other daughters

Ankhesenamun

Tutankhamun
1336–1327 BC

HE IS CROWNED...

Tutankhamun was probably brought up in Akhenaten's royal court at El-Armana. He became pharaoh, aged just nine, in 1336 BC, and was crowned at Memphis.

MARRIES...

Tutankhamun married his half-sister, Ankhesenamun. They had no children who survived, though two foetuses found in the tomb may have been their stillborn daughters.

RULES EGYPT...

Because Tutankhamun was just a boy, he was very dependent on his ministers. Most important decisions were taken by Ay, the elderly chief minister, and Horemheb, the head of the army.

Akhenaten

TUTANKHAMUN'S FATHER, AKHENATEN, introduced a new religion, the worship of the sun disc, or Aten. He banned the other gods and closed their temples. These changes were unpopular – ordinary people could no longer worship the traditional gods, and the priests lost their power.

The heretic pharaoh
After his death, Akhenaten was considered a heretic (someone whose religious views are unacceptable), and officials tried to destroy all mention of his name and those of his successors – Smenkhkare, Tutankhamun, and Ay.

Ruins at El-Amarna
Akhenaten built a new capital city, called Akhetaten, at the site now known as El-Amarna. The city once had palaces, a temple to the Aten, and houses for the nobles, but it was abandoned soon after Akhenaten's death. These ruins are all that is left.

Worshipping the Aten
According to Akhenaten, the Aten was the only god. The Aten created and cared for mankind and could be reached only by the pharaoh. In this carving (left), Akhenaten, Nefertiti, and some of their six daughters are receiving light rays from the Aten. Each ray ends in the *ankh* symbol, which means "life".

Nefertiti
Akhenaten's queen was the beautiful Nefertiti. She was very powerful, but after the thirteenth year of the king's reign she is no longer mentioned. Was she dead or disgraced? Or, as some evidence suggests, did she take a new name and become the mysterious Smenkhkare?

Bust of Nefertiti by a sculptor named Djehutemose

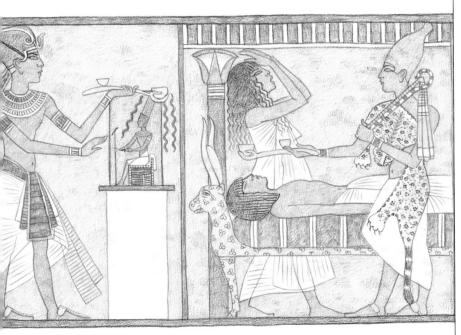

RESTORES RELIGION...
The young king reintroduced the worship of Amun and the other gods. As a sign of this, he changed his name from its earlier version, Tutankhaten, to Tutankhamun.

AND DIES
Tutankhamun died suddenly in 1327 BC, the ninth year of his reign. He was succeeded by Ay, who may have thought this was his last chance to seize the throne.

Was he murdered?

TWO POST MORTEMS have been carried out on Tutankhamun's corpse. Neither could prove the cause of death, but damage to the skull suggested that he either had an accident or was hit on the head. Some experts believe that Ay had Tutankhamun murdered so that he could be pharaoh.

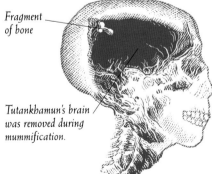

Fragment of bone

Tutankhamun's brain was removed during mummification.

X-ray of Tutankhamun's skull
This X-ray, taken in 1968, shows a piece of bone inside the skull. This could have been caused by a fall, a blow to the head, or the mummification process. Recent evidence suggests a blow was the most likely. So Tutankhamun was probably murdered.

MUMMIES AND EMBALMING

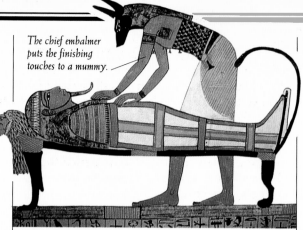

The chief embalmer puts the finishing touches to a mummy.

T HE EGYPTIANS BELIEVED THAT TO LIVE FOR ever in the afterlife, they had to preserve the body. They thought that everyone had several spirits. The most important were the *ka*, the body's spirit double, and the *ba*, the essence of the person's personality. These spirits would need a body to inhabit in the afterlife, so the dead body was preserved by embalming it.

The embalmers
The chief embalmer was called the "controller of the mysteries" and was often depicted as Anubis, the god of embalming. His many assistants included the lector priest, who recited spells throughout the process.

1 PURIFICATION
When someone died, the embalmers at once took the body away to the *ibu*, the "tent of purification". There they began the complicated process of embalming the body. While the lector priest read spells out loud, other priests carried out the first stage – cleaning the body with natron (a form of salt) dissolved in water.

Scenes from a coffin
The Egyptians did not leave many pictures of the embalming process. These rare scenes are taken from the painted coffin of Djedbastiufankh, who died in about 600 BC.

Priests carry out the cleansing of the body, pouring natron and water over it again and again.

2 REMOVAL OF THE CANOPIC ORGANS
After cleansing, the body was taken to the *wabet*, "the place of embalming". The next task was to take out certain internal organs. One priest, "the scribe", marked the line of a long cut on the lower left side of the stomach, then another, called "the slicer" cut the body open. The stomach, intestines, lungs, and liver were then removed.

Ceremonial knife
The "slicer" priest used a flint knife like this one. As soon as he had finished, he was driven away by the other priests, in case his act had offended the gods.

3 BRAIN AND HEART
The brain was pulled out through the nose with special hooks, which were pushed up one nostril and into the skull. The heart was left in the body, because the dead person would need it when he or she was judged by Osiris (see page 38).

Heart scarab
An amulet (charm) of a scarab beetle was placed over the heart to protect it against the perils of the underworld.

These hooks were used to pull out the brain.

4 DRYING THE BODY
Next, the body was dried out completely. Natron was packed into the abdomen, then the body was laid on a bed with more natron laid around it. The bed was often slightly tilted, so that any fluids could drain away. The drying process took 40 days.

From death to the funeral
Herodotus wrote that the dead body was dried in natron for 70 days. Historians now think that 70 days was the period from the person's death to the funeral. All the stages of mummification had to be completed within this time, as shown below.

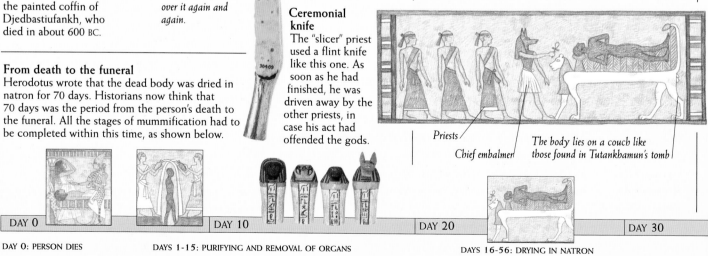

Priests

Chief embalmer

The body lies on a couch like those found in Tutankhamun's tomb

| DAY 0 | DAY 10 | DAY 20 | DAY 30 |

DAY 0: PERSON DIES   DAYS 1-15: PURIFYING AND REMOVAL OF ORGANS   DAYS 16-56: DRYING IN NATRON

5 ANOINTING

After 40 days, the body was washed to remove the natron, then taken to the *per nefer*, the "beautiful house", for anointing. Here, the abdomen was stuffed with clay, sawdust, or other materials, then the skin was massaged with perfumes and oils to make it flexible.

Bag of natron
Natron was a mixture of salts, including sodium carbonate and sodium bicarbonate. It was found around the edges of desert lakes.

6 BANDAGING

Next the body was covered in melted resin. It was then ready for bandaging. Using strips of linen, first the head, then each toe and finger, then the arms and legs, and finally the trunk were painstakingly wrapped. The bandages were kept tight and coated with resin to stiffen them.

Canopic jars

Bandaging was usually done by lesser priests, but overseen by the chief embalmer.

Shroud
The final layer was a shroud – a large piece of linen that covered the entire body. It was held in place by a long bandage running from head to toe.

7 MASK

The mummy's face was covered with a mask. This was a portrait of the dead person, which would help the *ba* spirit to recognize its body. Ordinary people had masks made from cartonnage, a mix of linen or plaster stiffened with resin.

Gold mask
Tutankhamun's mask was made of two layers of beaten gold, inlaid with semi-precious stones.

8 COFFINS

Finally, the completed mummy was laid in a coffin, or in several coffins, one inside another. This was both for protection and to provide a place for the *ka* spirit to rest. Coffins were mummy-shaped and usually made of painted or gilded wood.

Tutankhamun's coffins
Tutankhamun's mummy lay in three coffins. The outer two were made of gilded wood, but the third was made from beaten gold.

Canopic jars

THE FOUR ORGANS that had been removed from the body were embalmed separately, then stored in four special containers, called canopic jars. Each jar was protected by one of the four sons of the god Horus – the lid of the jar was often in the shape of the god's head.

Pharaoh's canopic jars
Tutankhamun's canopic organs were placed in beaten gold coffinettes.

Stomach
The stomach was placed in the jar with the jackal head of Duamutef. This jar was also protected by the goddess Neith.

Lungs
The god Hapy, who had the head of a baboon, protected the lungs. This jar was linked to the goddess Nephthys.

Liver
The liver was guarded by the god Imsety, who had a human head. The goddess Isis looked after this canopic jar.

Intestines
The falcon-headed god, Qebehsenuef looked after the intestines. This jar was under the protection of the goddess Selkis.

HERODOTUS

Much of what we know about embalming comes from the writings of the ancient Greek historian, Herodotus. He visited Egypt in about 450 BC. and watched embalmers at work.

Herodotus' account
"As much as possible of the brain is extracted through the nostrils with an iron hook... next the flank is laid open with a flint knife and the contents of the abdomen removed; the cavity is then thoroughly cleansed... After that it is filled with myrrh, cassia, and every other aromatic substance...after which the body is placed in natron, covered entirely over, for 70 days – never longer. When this period is over, the body is washed and wrapped from head to foot in linen cut into strips."

DAY 40	DAY 50	DAY 60	DAY 70

DAYS 57-58: ANOINTING   DAYS 59-69: BANDAGING   DAY 70: FUNERAL

THE ARCHAEOLOGISTS AT WORK

WHEN TUTANKHAMUN'S TOMB WAS FOUND, everyone thought it would be cleared and its contents displayed within a few weeks. With many other archaeologists of that time, this would have happened – and most of the objects might have been damaged beyond repair. But Carter was different. He and his team took the utmost care to protect the treasures, and to keep proper records of their discovery. As a result, it took them 10 years to clear the tomb.

Engrossed in his work
Carter wrote: "It was slow work... and nerve-wracking at that". Here, he is cleaning the face of the second coffin with a paintbrush.

1 PHOTOGRAPHS

Before anything was touched, Harry Burton photographed each room, showing the exact position of everything in it. Then he placed a numbered card on each object and photographed the room again. Each item could then be identified by its number.

Numbered objects in the antechamber
The objects were photographed in groups, with each number appearing in at least one picture. A photograph of each item was filed with Carter's notes to show where the object was found.

From discovery to museum
The tomb was discovered in 1922, but it was 1932 before the last of the treasures was safely sent to the museum in Cairo. It took Carter two-and-a-half years to clear the burial chamber alone. Some of the main events of the clearance are shown on the timeline below.

2 SKETCHES

Carter's artistic skills were to prove very useful. He made what he called "sketches" of many of the items found in the tomb. These were actually very precise drawings. He also kept notes about each object, recording its size, where it was found, what it was made of, and details of any inscriptions.

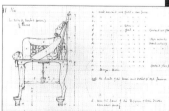

Carter's records
Carter made his preliminary notes and drawings on graph paper. This is his record of Tutankhamun's golden throne (see page 33).

3 REMOVING THE TREASURES

The treasures had to be carried out of the tomb with great care. Each item was tied with bandages to a padded wooden stretcher. When a number of stretchers were ready, they were carried under guard to the nearby tomb of Sety II. Large items, such as the animal couches and chariots found in the antechamber, had to be taken to pieces first.

The chest was secured to the stretcher with bandages.

Removing a chest
Each time an object was carried out, it caused great excitement among the crowd of press and tourists who waited constantly outside the tomb.

4 NOVEMBER 1922
TOMB DISCOVERED

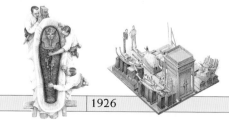

1922	1923	1924	1925	1926

DECEMBER 1922
WORK STARTED IN ANTECHAMBER

16 FEBRUARY 1923
OPENING OF BURIAL CHAMBER

11 NOVEMBER 1925
POST MORTEM BEGUN

24 OCTOBER 1926
WORK STARTED IN TREASURY